ink

Here We Go Looby Loo

Distributed by The Child's World®
1980 Lookout Drive • Mankato, MN 56003-1705
800-599-READ • www.childsworld.com

Acknowledgments
The Child's World®: Mary Berendes, Publishing Director
The Design Lab: Kathleen Petelinsek, Design

Library of Congress Cataloging-in-Publication Data
Freeman-Hines, Laura.
 Here we go looby loo / illustrated by Laura Freeman.
    p. cm.
 ISBN 978-1-60954-291-7 (library bound: alk. paper)
 1. Children's songs, English—Texts. [1. Songs. 2. Singing games.
 3. Games.] I. Title.
 PZ8.3.F9067He 2011
 782.42—dc22
 [E]   2010032427

Printed in the United States of America in Mankato, Minnesota.
December 2010
PA02074

ILLUSTRATED BY LAURA FREEMAN

Here we go looby loo.

Here we go looby light.

Here we go looby loo,

all on a Saturday night.

I put my right hand in.

I put my right hand out.

I give my hand
a shake, shake, shake . . .

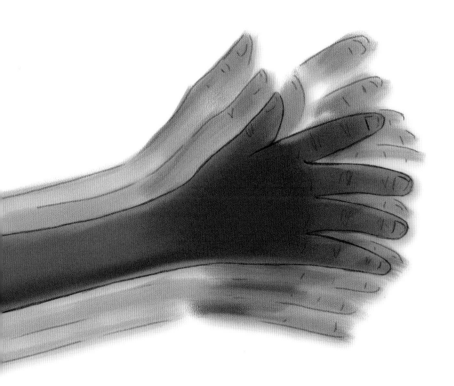

. . . and turn
myself about!

SONG ACTIVITY

Here we go looby loo.
Here we go looby light.
Here we go looby loo,
all on a Saturday night.
I put my right hand in.
I put my right hand out.
I give my hand a shake, shake, shake
and turn myself about!

Have everyone stand in a circle and sing the song.
When it comes to the words "I put my right hand in,"
everyone puts their right hand in the middle of the
circle. Everyone takes their hands out of the circle and
shakes their hand when the words of the song reach
those parts. Continue the song using your left hand,
your right foot, and then your left foot!

BENEFITS OF NURSERY RHYMES AND ACTIVITY SONGS

Activity songs and nursery rhymes are more than just a fun way to pass the time. They are a rich source of intellectual, emotional, and physical development for a young child. Here are some of their benefits:

❁ Learning the words and activities builds the child's self-confidence—"I can do it all by myself!"

❁ The repetitious movements build coordination and motor skills.

❁ The close physical interaction between adult and child reinforces both physical and emotional bonding.

❁ In a context of "fun," the child learns the art of listening in order to learn.

❁ Learning the words expands the child's vocabulary. He or she learns the names of objects and actions that are both familiar and new.

❁ Repeating the words helps develop the child's memory.

❁ Learning the words is an important step toward learning to read.

❁ Reciting the words gives the child a grasp of English grammar and how it works. This enhances the development of language skills.

❁ The rhythms and rhyming patterns sharpen listening skills and teach the child how poetry works. Eventually the child learns to put together his or her own simple rhyming words— "I made a poem!"

ABOUT THE ILLUSTRATOR

Laura Freeman has been drawing pictures for as long as she can remember, and illustrating books since 1998. She's from New York City, but currently lives in Atlanta with her husband, their two children, and a very small hamster.